Mantra & Yantra

BIHAR SCHOOL OF YOGA

50 years

1963–2013
GOLDEN JUBILEE

WORLD YOGA CONVENTION 2013
GANGA DARSHAN, MUNGER, BIHAR, INDIA
23rd–27th October 2013

Mantra & Yantra

Swami Niranjanananda Saraswati

*Discourses from the Yogadrishti (Yogavision) series of satsangs
held at Ganga Darshan Vishwa Yogapeeth, Chandhisthana and
Dashbhujisthana, Munger, during Chaitra Navaratri,
17th to 20th March 2010*

Yoga Publications Trust, Munger, Bihar, India

Published by Yoga Publications Trust
    First edition 2010
    Reprinted 2012

ISBN: 978-81-86336-86-1

Publisher and distributor: Yoga Publications Trust, Ganga Darshan, Munger, Bihar, India.

Website: www.biharyoga.net
        www.rikhiapeeth.net

Printed at Aegean Offset Printers, Greater Noida

Dedication

*To our guru Sri Swami Satyananda Saraswati
who continues to inspire and guide us
on our spiritual journey.*

Contents

Origin of Mantra

17th March 2010

Space and creation

In the scriptures, space is known as Brahman. *Kham Brahman* is the statement of the Vedas. *Kham* means space and *Brahman* means the all-pervasive reality.

In Samkhya philosophy space is also an element. This element is the foundation and basis for the development and emergence of all other elements and forms of creation. Space is immeasurable. It cannot be measured, no matter at which point of space you are. If you want to know the centre of space, you can be in any quadrant of space, and that will always be the centre for you. Distances do not matter in space; they exist and are immeasurable. Space is infinite, and this infinitely vast element, or *tattwa*, has been called Brahman.

Brahman means the all-pervasive reality, and space is where the forces of the cosmos and the universe, energies and different worlds, exist in harmony with each other. They are the essence of the space tattwa in their latent form.

The prime essence of the space tattwa is consciousness and energy; consciousness and energy become Brahman, the all-pervasive reality. Consciousness + energy = all-pervasive reality, which is known as Brahman. The essence is inherent in space, and space is infinite, without any boundaries. Just as a fire flame is not separate from its heat, consciousness and

1

energy are not separate from the space element. In tantra, this consciousness has been called Shiva and the energy has been called Shakti. In Vedanta they have been called Brahman and Maya; in Samkhya, Purusha and Prakriti. Just as the shadow remains hidden in the body, in that eternal, endless space, consciousness remains inherent in the form of Shiva, Brahman or Purusha, and energy remains hidden in the form of Shakti, Maya or Prakriti.

In the material dimension, the reflection of consciousness and energy is perceived in our life, in the form of mind and body, or mind and matter. The mind is a reflection of that infinite consciousness, but it is not infinite consciousness, just as your reflection in the mirror is not you. In space the consciousness is infinite, but in the body one is limited by the senses. At the physical level it is expressed through the agencies of the mind and the senses. In the transcendental form, consciousness is the essence which is all-pervasive, and in the manifest form consciousness is the mind: the total mind, higher mind, complete mind or individual consciousness. Energy, which is also the essence of space, becomes matter in the manifest dimension. The body of matter is the gross form of that energy. Thus, what is 'out there' is reflected in our life in the form of mind and matter.

In space these two qualities are totally balanced and in harmony with each other. The state of harmony is where the essential nature remains stabilized in itself. For example, if you cut a seed into pieces, you will not see leaves, flowers and fruits, but the potency of all these exists in the seed. This potency exists in the seed in the form of its qualities, and these qualities are not in conflict with each other, but in harmony. While the seed remains a seed, the potency remains hidden in harmony. When it associates with earth, air and light, there is a change in its essential nature, and the seed sprouts. Now, the *gunas* or qualities are no longer in a state of harmony in the seed – one quality is stronger, another weaker, and so on. Qualitatively, wood, leaves and flowers are all different. Each has a different nature and qualities.

2

Wood and a flower have completely opposite qualities, but in seed form no difference is perceived. The differences become visible only upon manifestation. Therefore, the state of harmony is like the state of the seed, where all possibilities exist equally.

In the cosmic dimension, while consciousness and energy are in a state of harmony and balance, creation does not take place. However, when consciousness and energy begin to interact with each other, then life and all the experiences of life manifest. When a *vikara*, or modification, takes place, when a transformation occurs due to the combination and permutation of these two forces, creation manifests. Creation is a vikara, an evolute of the permutation and combination of consciousness and energy.

Experiencing consciousness and energy

Consciousness and energy manifest as life in the form of spirit, mind, senses, intellect and ego. The two are present in every aspect of creation in the form of *ashta prakriti*, the eight-fold aspects of manifest nature, consisting of the five senses and the three attributes of the mind: *manas*, the reasoning mind, *buddhi*, the intellect, and *ahamkara*, the ego identity. Therefore, it is said that God exists everywhere; that Supreme Element exists in every atom, type of matter, form and state.

From the Indian philosophical perspective, God is not a person or a figure, but rather an experience. For example, air is invisible. You cannot see air, unlike earth, water and fire which are visible elements. Yet the different manifestations of air have each been given a name and identity. Sometimes air is a cool breeze, sometimes a storm, a typhoon or a tornado.

What do these names indicate about what cannot be seen by the eyes? They indicate manifestations which you are able to experience and feel. You cannot see air, but you can experience it, identify the sensation, the feeling, the knowledge, the understanding and the awareness of it, and give it a name: a cool breeze. The term 'cool breeze' indicates your understanding of an experience of the movement of the air.

The ancient seers believed that life is nothing but an expression of consciousness and energy. Mind and matter are the manifestations of consciousness and energy. Shiva and Shakti, Purusha and Prakriti, Brahman and Maya exist in a form which is all-pervasive. There is not a single part of creation which is devoid of the influence of consciousness and energy. They manifest in myriad forms, not only in forms recognizable as human beings or animals or insects.

4

In our life, the experience of consciousness and energy takes place in the form of mind and matter. Mind is the subtle content or form of consciousness. Matter is the manifest gross form of energy. The same consciousness and energy which pervade the entire creation also exist in life in the form of mind and matter. In their cosmic form they are transcendental; in their manifest form they are bound by limitations placed by life, by the mind, senses, ego, and by creation.

When we try to identify powers that are beyond human perception and comprehension, we refer to them as being beyond the human rationale and unable to be grasped by the human mind. However, when the mind begins to experience these powers, then an identity is perceived. After all, your mind goes through different experiences which you can identify as a belief, a thought, a desire, an aspiration, an ambition or a motivation. These are different awarenesses and impressions of the mind which can be identified. Can you identify the mind? People say no. People need a medium through which they can access the mind, realize the mind and be aware of the mind. The medium which makes one aware of the mind can be a single thought, an emotion, a desire, an understanding or a motivation – all the varied expressions of the mind. When feeling hate, you are experiencing your mind. When feeling love, you are experiencing your mind. When feeling compassion or aggression, you are experiencing your mind. Just as a medium is needed to experience the mind, in order to realize the influence and effect of the cosmic powers of consciousness and energy, one needs to know the medium through which they express themselves in the material world.

Consciousness assumes the form of the mind and becomes the observer. Consciousness is never active; its nature is stillness. Energy is active; it is the basis of creation. Without energy, creation cannot happen. Without energy, there would be no sun, moon, stars or life – nothing. Energy, or Shakti, is the predominant factor in creation and in experiencing life. Consciousness is used to realize the different manifestations and influences of Shakti. Consciousness identifies the mood of Shakti and acts accordingly. For example, when you are agitated, consciousness recognizes the agitation, but it is energy that controls your body. When there is fear, consciousness recognizes fear, but it is energy manifesting as fear. The same is true of all other emotions. This Shakti or energy has been identified by different names, according to the expression and experience of the individual.

In the Indian tradition, one of the identities that this energy has been visualized as is the form of Devi. The Devi image is a symbolic representation to understand and identify a state, a change and a process. The term 'devi', which is used to identify transformative forces, is derived from the root *div*, which means self-illumined. These forces are self-illuminated; they are complete in themselves.

The three main cosmic powers that guide the created dimension and life have been realized as Durga, Lakshmi and Saraswati. Durga is *kriya shakti*, the power of action, Lakshmi is *ichcha shakti*, the power of will, and Saraswati is *jnana shakti*, the power of wisdom. Life is realized between birth and death. On one side is birth, one cosmic force, on the other side is death, another cosmic force, and in the middle is life, a third cosmic force. At the time of birth it is Saraswati power. At the time of death it is Durga power. In between birth and death the force that nourishes life is Lakshmi power. For example: you require office space. You locate a building. It is new, ready to be leased out. You select your office space in the building. When you receive the space it is empty, not even clean, full of dust and cobwebs. What do you do first? Clean the office. What do you do next? Bring in your furniture and arrange it the way you want it and then decorate your office according to your preference. When all this is done, on a given day you enter your office, sit down at your desk and begin work. This example indicates the application of the three powers in the simple process of acquiring an office space.

The first power is Durga. She cleans, removes all the dirt and cobwebs and gives you the energy to open the windows which allows in the sunlight and fresh air. She gives you the inspiration and strength to clean the room thoroughly. This is kriya shakti. Once the room is cleaned, then Lakshmi power takes over. You bring in your furniture and decorate the office; you make yourself comfortable, secure and happy. Ichcha shakti is primary and kriya shakti assists the attainment of ichcha. Once the ichcha or Lakshmi power has completed its run, Saraswati power takes over. On a given day you inaugurate the office, sit down and start your work. You begin to add to your knowledge and understanding by jnana shakti. This is the application of the three shaktis.

Durga is that aspect of cosmic power which helps one overcome, transcend and transform the limitations and

negativities of life. The word *durgam* means difficult, and *durga* means one who eases the difficulties. If you had to convert a barren piece of land into a produce farm, what difficulties would you encounter and what would you do to facilitate the conversion of the land? You would start digging the land first, remove the weeds, grass, stones and rocks, and prepare the soil. Such a change from a given state to another state is the Durga component. Until we give the land a shape which will be finally utilized for farming, the whole exercise is one of Durga power.

Next, you start working on the field, planting crops and looking after them with the hope that they will one day nourish you and also earn you some money – this idea of prosperity, security and comfort is the Lakshmi concept. Afterwards, when the crops are harvested and you are enjoying the results of your effort, and feel happy and contented, that is the Saraswati concept.

Durga represents change, transformation and the preparation made to cultivate something new. Durga is not an aggressive energy, but a benevolent energy preparing the ground for change. However, even benevolence needs to have some force and power; it needs some aggressive power for it to establish itself. Power and benevolence, the destructive force and the benevolent force are both seen in Durga. She is depicted as holding different weapons in her ten hands, which are symbolic representations. When you need to bring about a change in your life and attain a new state, when you wish to leave the old behind and acquire the new, you need certain weapons, methods to accomplish this. The weapons in Durga's hands represent methods to transform the negative qualities in life.

Lakshmi eases the passage through life by bestowing happiness, security, contentment and fulfilment, and by removing that which we lack in life and making us full. Lakshmi sustains and nourishes. She does not hold any weapons in her hands – only a lotus and a pot of gold, representing auspiciousness and prosperity. Only when there is physical, mental, and spiritual wellbeing and prosperity can one attain wisdom and bliss. Finally, when one enjoys the fruit of action, feeling contented, in bliss – that is Saraswati, depicted as holding a book and a veena. These are the three main attributes of that cosmic energy and consciousness, which are realized in life as Durga – death, transformation or change, Lakshmi – continuation, and Saraswati – birth. The sequence of the three processes: change, stability and realization of one's potential, culminating in bliss, is achieved through the invocation of these shaktis.

The ancient rishis realized that it is possible to awaken these three cosmic forces within us. It is possible to generate an awareness of energy and harness and channel that power for our upliftment. Therefore, when the yogis were exploring and realizing these shaktis, they were researching their own consciousness and trying to discover solutions to the distresses of life. They did not have any religious ideology in mind. They were bent on discovering a connection between human beings and the cosmic nature.

In the process of accessing their psyche, they utilized mantra and yantra. Mantra and yantra constitute the instruments, mediums or methods by which one can explore and realize energy patterns and awaken the dormant centres of consciousness. Mantras and yantras are not only a combination of sounds and visual images used in meditation, but represent the first subtle manifestation of the two cosmic powers of consciousness and energy, as mantra and yantra.

Primal sound

The first subtle manifestation in creation is sound. Sound is the manifestation of consciousness and energy in their purest form. However, the sound that we hear through the ears or record with an instrument is gross, material noise. Subtle sound exists in the form of a *spandan*, vibration. Whenever there is any kind of permutation or combination, a third result is always seen which, in the case of consciousness and

energy, is vibration or spandan. That is the first evolute, the first manifestation.

This idea has been conveyed in many world cultures. The Old Testament of the Bible states, "In the beginning was the word, and the word was with God." What is the meaning of this statement? "In the beginning was the word" means that the subtle vibration, the spandan, has always existed because of the permutation and combination of consciousness and energy. Similarly, in the tantric systems, *Shiva Charitra* describes the emergence of the world. It is said that Shiva, the transcendental consciousness, manifests in the world in the form of sound, vibration. That sound, that vibratory body, is called *shabda sharira*.

When the basic structure of the universe was created, when the stars, planets and earth were formed, there was no life. At that moment the Creator and the Preserver, Brahma and Vishnu were arguing about their roles in creation. To bring a stop to their argument, a *nada*, or primal sound, manifested, like the sound of an explosion. That sound has been called God's shabda sharira. What emerged thereafter was a *jyotirlingam*, an effulgent lingam, which had neither a beginning nor an end. That was the *prakashmaya sharira* of God, the body of light. Thus, first to manifest was the vibratory body and then came the light body. The light body has been called linga sharira, for it is visualized in the form of a lingam, and the lingam is symbolic of the formless, transcendental God.

The sound that manifested was *Aum*: 'A' 'U' 'M'. *Aum* represents the primal sound, the primal vibration. The three syllables 'A', 'U' and 'M' indicate the growth and emergence of *bhasha*, language. In any language the first letter is always A, whether it be Greek, English, Hindi or Arabic. That is the base sound. All other sounds have emerged after 'A'. If you put the sound 'M' at the end of any letter, it indicates the end of that sound wave. The middle is 'U'; it is a link between 'A' and 'M'. These three syllables, 'A', 'U', 'M' also represent the three shaktis, the three gunas, the three states of consciousness, the three lokas, in fact, the trinity inherent in creation.

The sound of *Aum* came as a revelation, not as an auditory experience. When it was revealed, you did not exist, I did not exist, life forms did not exist. *Aum* was a revelation as the sound inherent in the universe and cosmos, as the sound which represents the higher transcendental reality, as the first expression and manifestation of the transcendental reality.

Science of vibration

The entire universe is moving, vibrating and pulsating. Pulsation indicates expansion and contraction. The entire universe is pulsating not only externally but also internally. In our own atomic structure there is pulsation of the nucleus within the atom which is vibrating and moving in space by itself. It is not moving on any defined axis, but pulsating and vibrating in space.

According to the science of vibration, *spanda shastra*, vibration is always caused by movement. If there is no

11

movement, no activity, no motion, then there will be stillness. Vibration will not be caused by a still situation. Therefore, vibration always indicates motion. Whether you are able to perceive it with your senses or not is a different matter, but vibration always accompanies motion, movement, action, merger or separation. This becomes the first *kriya*, the first act, of consciousness and energy.

Similarly, when universes, galaxies and solar systems are formed, the planets create their own sounds, noise and vibrations. These are the nadas of the planets, a fact that has also been proven now. Spacecrafts like Voyagers, which have gone beyond our solar system, have captured sounds from different planets as they have flown past. Whatever these sounds may be, some motion or action is taking place there. As everything moves around, the infinite space which seems silent is actually full of noise and vibration, full of sound.

It is the same within the body. Therefore, the Upanishads say that what is outside is reflected in the body. Outside is the macro-universe and this body is the micro-universe. This matter which relates to the body is a replica or reflection of the macro-universe. In your body there are infinite sounds, vibrations and noises, but the agent, the medium, the instrument of the auditory faculty picks up sounds within a certain range. However, if you were able to cultivate the ability to hear the higher and lower ranges of sounds, you would be surprised to find that there is a full symphony orchestra playing inside you.

This is the subject of the science of vibration as defined by the tantras. Tantra is the only system which has defined the science of vibration. The school of Kashmir Shaivism has many theories on the subject of vibration, which the yogis realized in states of deep meditation.

Dissipated mind
The normal state of mind is dissipated, not focused or one-pointed. Where the mind goes we don't even know, even now you are not aware of where your mind has gone. One moment

you are listening to me, the other moment there is a gap – where did your mind go at that time? What happened to your awareness and attention? Why did that gap come in your awareness? And this happens practically every minute. Just to hold the awareness at one point for two minutes is difficult. When you do your mantra japa, for how many beads are you aware of the mantra, and at which point do you forget that you are moving the beads or repeating the mantra? There is a lapse of awareness, and it happens because of the extroverted nature of the senses and mind.

When the mind and senses are extroverted, then subtle awareness is not there. Subtle awareness means focused awareness. You are listening to me right now. If twenty loudspeakers come on at the same time with different types of music, your mind will be totally distracted. You will not be able to focus on what I am saying. In order to focus you need to block out all other sounds and then you will be able to listen to my voice. If you are unable to block out the other sounds, the noise will not allow you to listen to what I am saying. Thus, in normal life when we meditate, we are only dealing with the lower mind and we cannot have higher experiences in meditation.

Higher mind awareness

From the yogic perspective the total mind is divided in two parts: the lower mind and the higher mind. The lower mind is subject to time, space and object, senses and sense objects, sense and sense associations, mind and mental associations, emotions and emotional associations. The higher mind is intuitive, peaceful, luminous and transcendental.

When we are practising meditation, we are able to access only the lower mind, to analyze and become aware of the lower behaviours of *manas*, the reasoning mind, *buddhi*, intelligence, *chitta*, memories, and *ahamkara*, ego identity. If we experience a little bit of peace, happiness and comfort in the lower mind, we feel that we have attained a good meditative state. Nobody can go beyond the lower mind in meditation. In order to go beyond the lower mind, drastic changes have to take place in one's life. One has to be a sannyasin of the same calibre as Swami Sivananda, Swami Satyananda and other such luminaries.

People who have drastically changed their mental structure, their social, physical, emotional and intellectual structure, don't function in the same dimension as any of us. They live in the higher mind and their association with the world is different from our association with the world. Their dealing with situations is different from our dealing with situations. Their comprehension, understanding and wisdom are different from our comprehension, understanding and wisdom.

When the yogis heard the mantras, when they realized the existence of vibrations at the universal level and experienced the same vibrations within them, they were in the state of meditation in the higher mind. At that level of higher mind awareness, there were no senses and association with sense objects to restrict their attainments. That is the state of dhyana or the state of samadhi.

The states of dhyana and samadhi are attained when the mind is not restricted by the influences of the senses and sense objects, when the mind is not bound by the influences of situations or attachments, but is totally free.

Realization of the vibratory body

When the mind is not affected by external conditions, it is connected with the vibratory body. From the yogic perspective, there are five different bodies that one experiences: *annamaya kosha*, the dimension of matter; *pranamaya kosha*, the dimension of energy; *manomaya kosha*, the dimension of mind; *vijnanamaya kosha*, the dimension of consciousness; and *anandamaya kosha*, the dimension of spirit. Involvement in the first three levels, annamaya, pranamaya and mano-maya koshas, indicates involvement with the lower mind. The higher mind is vijnanamaya kosha, the unrestrained, unrestricted consciousness, and anandamaya kosha, which

14

is actually the vibratory body. Spiritual awareness, the dimension of spirit is the dimension of vibrations.

As spiritual aspirants, as yoga aspirants, we can go up to an understanding of the lower mind, but beyond that we need to have access to our inner nature in order to experience the subtle aspects of consciousness and vibrations. When the yogis entered into deep meditation after perfecting their own sadhana, they did not see an image of God revealing itself before their eyes. What was revealed to them was the essence: consciousness and energy. What was revealed were the evolutes of this essence of life: the vibrations, the elements, the tattwas, the gross nature, the pancha bhootas, the pancha tattwas, the tanmatras, manas, buddhi, chitta, ahamkara, the senses, etc. This was the realization of the yogis.

The yogis did not meditate to realize God, because for yogis God is formless. If I believe, that is my personal belief. If you believe, that is your personal belief. But as far as the tradition is concerned the understanding of God is open. If you read the *Yoga Sutras* of Patanjali, it simply says that God is a person with special attributes, attributes which we don't possess. God is endowed with special qualities which we don't possess. You are free to define what those attributes and qualities are, according to your conviction and choice. The philosophy of yoga does not impose the idea that God is like this or like that. Religions impose such ideas and people are drawn to different aspects of religions to enhance their own understanding of the experiences they are going through.

The yogis were not actually looking for God-realization when they were meditating. They were trying to discover the nature of life and creation. For them God was always *Kham Brahman* – infinite space, the container in which creation can take place. In meditation, when they transcended body awareness, mind awareness, sense awareness, object awareness and time awareness, and came to space awareness, there, they were able to perceive all the different vibrations that exist in the universe. These vibrations were given a name: mantra.

Etymology of 'mantra'

The word *mantra* was given to the vibrations as it means the power through which one can manage and free one's mind. Mantra is defined as *mananat trayate iti mantrah* – the power, force or energy through which one is able to liberate the mind from its obsessions is called mantra.

Why do yogis call these sound vibrations mantra? In the highest state of meditation, when the sound vibrations are revealing themselves to the yogi's mind, when the yogi's mind is functioning in harmony with the higher, universal energy frequencies, then sounds are heard in the form of spandan, vibration. There the vibration is in a state of equilibrium, but in the manifest dimension consciousness has manifested as mind, and energy as matter. Being a sound component beyond the human auditory range, the vibration exerts an influence on the mental behaviour. It is a different input from the normal mental masalas that have gone in to make up this structure.

16

One may cook vegetables, adding spices, salt and everything else in the preparation and bring it to the table. Now, if one then adds a spoonful of butter or ghee to it, the taste of the food is completely changed. Similarly, in this life you have come with prepared things, but the revelation of those higher vibrations is like adding butter or ghee to the sabji or dal. It changes the quality, the taste, it is no longer the same, it is not the original version; it becomes different. What becomes different? The conditionings, the mind, the body, the manifest state.

Power of mantra
At the cosmic level mantras are identified as vibration. At the gross level the vibrations are recognized as mantras. At the cosmic level spandan means vibration, and at the physical level the vibrations are translated in the form of mantras which affect the manifest nature, consciousness, and mind, matter and energy.

There are many parts of a mantra. Each mantra has a positive power and a negative power. Each mantra influences and awakens a particular area or centre of the mind and the brain. The positive power of the mantra is known as the deity of the mantra, and the negative power is known as the *ugra shakti* of the mantra. If you read the book *Kundalini Tantra* by Swami Satyananda, you will find that in a chakra the main power is the mantra, whether *Yam*, *Lam*, *Ram* and so on. Along with that you will find representations of Devi, the positive forces, the positive qualities of the mantra. You will also find images of dakinis, shakinis and rakinis, which are the violent tendencies of the mantra. A mantra can influence the water element, which means it will work on the mind. A mantra which influences the *agni* or fire element will work on prana. Each mantra is very specific; one mantra is not applicable to everyone. Therefore, when a mantra is being given, the personality of the aspirant has to be considered.

Each mantra affects a particular element, a *tattwa*. Each mantra has its positive power and negative power, each

17

mantra has its medium by which it can be awakened, and which is represented in the form of its vehicle. The elephant is the vehicle of the mantra of mooladhara chakra. The elephant represents a quality of the mind, the intellect. Therefore, the positive power of mooladhara is Ganesha, the power which overcomes obstacles – the drive, determination and motivation. If you are able to maintain the clarity of your motivation and drive, balance your intellect and manage the manifestations of mooladhara, you will be able to realize the effect of the mantra of mooladhara.

Perfecting mantra

The science of mantra is complex. You cannot just choose a mantra, or start analyzing your own: "Am I fire, am I water? Which is the air mantra, which is the fire mantra?" A mantra in itself is not only a sound or a vibration, but covers many different areas which you begin to experience as they are revealed to you during your sadhana. If you know exactly how to use the influences of the mantra to manage your mind, uplift your emotions and awaken your spiritual powers, then that is the right application of the mantra. This application is taught much further on in the spiritual journey between guru and disciple. Right now the mantra which you have is for your japa, it is for perfecting pratyahara. Don't expect to go beyond that until you are able to perfect mantra pratyahara.

When Sri Swamiji gave me my mantra, he told me to practise one mala every day. The mantra was small, so I used to finish my japa in five minutes. Some time later I said to him, "I am finishing my mantra japa in five minutes, can I increase the number of malas?" He said, "How much would you like to increase it?" I said, "Well, one mala takes me five minutes. I can easily increase it to five or six malas. At least half an hour of solid sitting would be good for me." He said, "You are thinking of solid sitting of the body. Tell me, is your awareness solid in the repetition of the mantra?" I said, "No." He said, "For how many beads of the mala are

18

you aware that you are repeating the mantra?" I said, "Maybe five, ten or twenty. And whenever I remember, I again bring my mind back." He said, "Then you have never completed a single mala in your life, and now you want to increase it to five. First finish one mala, which means total awareness for 108 mantras."

When Sri Swamiji was performing sadhana in Rikhia, he used to tell people, "Don't come to see me or talk to me, because if you come then I have to stop my sadhana and my mantra repetition in order to talk to you. If I can remain aware of my mantra for twenty-four hours of the day, that will be an attainment. If you come for two minutes the chain is broken. If you come for an hour's satsang, the chain is broken. So, don't come." If mantra awareness deepens, then one attains the highest spiritual realization. That is the training of the mind. You can't even do one mala! Therefore, for ordinary people like us, just one mala is enough. We have to increase our attention span on that.

So, yogis heard the mantras and discovered that they contained many other components such as a positive power, a negative power, an area of influence, an area of emergence. Then they developed the concept of chakras. They allotted different frequencies to different chakras. The chakras, which are symbolized in the spine, actually reflect an altered state of mind and matter, consciousness and energy.

The science of mantra is an incomparable gift by the Indian seers to the world. In no other culture will you find such an elaborate system of mantras. They are the medium through which, by understanding the connection of one's life with Nature and the Supreme Reality, one can act in accordance with Nature and make the effort towards self-realization.

Types of Mantra & Mantra Sadhana

18th March 2010

Sound is the link between the cosmos and the individual. The mind and body are a reflection of the supreme consciousness and supreme energy. This body is energy, not matter. It is perceived as matter, but it is only a gross form of energy. Vibration, which emerges from the interaction between consciousness and energy, also becomes the cause for union between the two in the individual unit. Mantra becomes the cause for the union of consciousness and prana. Consciousness and energy influence the mind in different ways at different times. When they manifest in an auspicious form, one experiences spirituality, divinity, love and compassion; there are inner visions of gods and goddesses, which are in fact the essential forms of consciousness.

You do not see air, but you give it a name based on your experience of its quality. In the same way, when this material mind crosses the limits of the senses and connects with that supreme consciousness and begins to experience it, then based on the experience it ascribes a form to it, whether it be Devi, Rama, Shiva or Vishnu. That Supreme Element becomes conscious for us in that form. This experience can take place with the help of mantra. The mantra is the medium, the rope with which we can climb out of the well of the world.

The scriptures state that as long as you are on level ground you can run wherever you like, but once you fall into a well your freedom ends. You have to stay within the periphery of the well. If you want to get out of the well, you will have to use a rope for support. It is the same with the individual soul. It is free in the unmanifest state, but when it enters the well of Prakriti, it becomes limited and bound. To emerge from this well, to free itself from the darkness of the well, to lift itself out of the limited state of the well, it needs a rope, and that rope is mantra.

Seed sounds

Sound is the first evolute, the first attribute that is perceived in the *akasha tattwa* or infinite space. This sound was perceived by yogis in higher states of meditation.

The yogis perceived three different ranges of sounds, or mantras. The first range is the ultra-low sound, the ultra-low vibration, the ultra-low frequency. It represents a state of balance between the tattwas at the cosmic level. Sounds heard in the ultra-low frequency range are not in the form of words, but in the form of nada. Sounds that have been identified as *Om, Hrim, Lam, Ram* or *Vam* fall into this category. These single-syllable sounds are called bija mantras.

When we repeat the mantra *Hrim* for Devi, or the mantra *Om*, it is a single-syllable sound that we are creating. It is just one letter. That letter in Sanskrit is called akshara. *Kshara* means that which decays or changes, and *akshara* means that which does not change, alter or decay. Therefore, the single-syllable bija mantras are aksharas, and they represent the transcendental *nada*, the transcendental vibration, which is beyond the human auditory range. It is a very deep resonance.

If there is a drum beat in the distance, the continuous resonance of that distant drum beat would be similar to the nada or bija mantra effect. Bija mantras are seed vibrations. *Bija* means seed, and just as a seed has an inherent potency for the development and growth of a tree, the latent potential of the mantra, its consciousness and power, are inherent in the seed sound.

22

Creation of sound

All sounds are vibrations. Sounds are created because of vibrations, even physiologically. How is sound produced by a human being? By air passing through the vocal cord. The vocal cord is so resilient that it can create any sound just by turning and twisting the lips and the tongue, by opening and closing the mouth. As air flows through the vocal cords a particular sound or vibration is created, which is heard by the sense organ of the ears. As sound is created by a material object, it is perceived by a material sense organ. When our vocal cords vibrate and create a sound, it is coming from an organ of the body. In order to hear that sound another organ of the body, the ears, are utilized.

The point is that just one vocal cord can generate different kinds of sound in many varieties, and each frequency, vibration and range of sound that emerges is different from the preceding or subsequent one. It is the same with bija mantras, which also modify different areas of the mind, brain and consciousness.

Power of sound

It has been the experience of yogis that with the practice of bhramari pranayama one acquires the ability of clairvoyance. You can see images of events that have not yet taken place. You can see visions and movies in your mind. This is a statement, but if you analyze the brahmari practice, you will understand the validity of the statement. The nada that is created during the practice of bhramari, the sustained sound of 'mmmmmmm', physically alters the brainwave patterns. It alters the energy fluctuations of the mind. It arrests the dissipations of the mind and the senses, and makes them focused.

An experiment was once conducted in a school. In a classroom about ten or fifteen grandfather clocks were placed, with the pendulums swinging at random. After a few hours it was discovered that all the pendulums were swinging in unison, moving in the same direction, in synchronicity, in harmony. At one point something happened which synchronized the movement of the pendulums. This phenomenon has been exlained as the effect of vibration. The physical object, the pendulum itself, is inert. It moves only because of the weight. At some point, the vibration being generated by the movement begins to affect the other movements, and they all eventually begin to move in unison. The same thing happens with mantra.

The humming sound of bhramari alters and synchronizes the brainwave patterns, the biorhythms of the body, and the dissipations of mental powers and energies, so that greater calmness, relaxation and concentration are experienced. It touches, stimulates or awakens a centre in the lower brain stem, which is the primitive brain. The primitive brain is affected by the resonance of the sound 'mmmmm' and it begins to trigger certain impulses, which alter the perceptions of the conscious mind.

When impulses are fired by the primitive brain, they do not go through the normal neural network of the brain which is much more organized than the primitive brain. So

24

where are they going? To some part which is influencing and altering our conscious perception. Therefore, visions and events are foreseen.

Some people attribute this to psychic powers and call it a *siddhi*. They do not understand the process of evolution or awakening. For them siddhis become miraculous powers. Siddhis are not miraculous powers; they are normal attainments of life. When you go to primary school, you do not know algebra, biology or history. However, when you have completed your studies, you have acquired the skills of algebra and are able to calculate formulas. For a child that would be miraculous, but not for you. For you it is only a sequential process that you have understood. In the same way, the science of mantra is a sequential process of harmonizing, integrating and awakening the experiences of the lower mind and the higher mind.

Mantras are vibrations which influence the elements: fire, water, air, earth and ether. In the 1970s, an experiment was conducted by scientists in a town in Uttar Pradesh in India. A thatched hut was built and it was completely empty except for sensitive temperature measuring instruments. It was checked for inflammable objects and then the police cordoned it off. A group of pandits and sadhus sat outside the hut and started chanting the *agni* (fire) mantra. As the chanting intensified, the temperature inside the hut started to rise, and was recorded by the instruments, to the extent that the hut eventually caught on fire. The mantra influenced the fire element.

If someone is depressed and they are asked to practise japa of the agni mantra, within a week they will be rid of depression. I once conducted an experiment in the USA when I was there in 1981–82. I visited a mental asylum which housed catatonic patients. The management asked me if these people could be helped. I thought about it. It wasn't possible for them to do yoga practices because they would not respond to any instructions to move their limbs. I had an idea. On my next visit I plugged their left nostrils with cotton

25

wool and instructed the hospital authorities not to remove the cotton wool. This meant that the patients would breathe only through the right nostril continuously. When I went back after three days, the patients had begun to move their limbs. By plugging the left nostril, ida nadi had been closed and pingala nadi was forced to become active. When the sun nadi becomes active, the pranas begin to vibrate, so that it is possible to get out of an extreme tamasic state. Next I gave them a tape on which I had chanted the agni mantra, *Ram*, the bija mantra of manipura chakra, 108 times. I asked the hospital to play the tape continuously. Within three months the patients were able to move their limbs and do their own chores.

To alter the perceptions of the conscious mind is not difficult. Yoga says that you can do this through meditation, through *aushadhi* or herbs, or other agents. Of course, now people look at the use of such herbs as an addiction or habit, but initially everything in creation supported the development of a particular state of existence. Drugs, whether marijuana, ganja or bhang, create an altered state of perception and are used for enjoyment and pleasure. However, when they are utilized to explore the realms of energy and consciousness, they can become very powerful tools, as long as there is control. In the past this is how yogis used them, and do so even today. Not for any other purpose except meditation – development of concentration and connection of one state of mind with another state of mind.

Rishi Valmiki, who was a dacoit, was asked to do *ulta japa*, reverse japa, to chant *Mara, Mara* instead of *Rama, Rama*. He could not pronounce *Rama*, so he was asked to say *Mara*. However, when he went on repeating *Mara, Mara*, it became *Rama, Rama*. This is the play of syllables. Valmiki's example also proves that when the mind becomes engrossed in a vibration, it is influenced by the mantra. He wasn't influenced by the word *Mara*, but the effect was that of the mantra *Rama*. If he had continued to repeat *Mara, Mara* he would only have had visions of dead bodies, for *mara* means dead. Every word

has a form and a quality, and it is possible that at first this was the image that appeared before Valmiki. However, as his identification with the mantra deepened, that form and quality disappeared from the name, and the name changed. It became *Rama*. When it became *Rama*, a new form and quality emerged in which there was a glimpse and realization of tranquillity and peace.

The Rama mantra is a mantra of peace and tranquillity. If you wish to change a restless state of mind to a peaceful state, chant the Rama mantra for five minutes, even if Rama is not your ishta. Don't look at these things from a religious point of view, but understand what is beneficial in your life. If you are sitting in your office and feeling restless, dissipated and upset, chant the Rama mantra for five minutes and you will experience peace and calm. If you are stuck in a state of laziness and feeling low in energy, chant the mantra *Ram*, without the long 'a' sound. Being the seed sound of the fire element, it will immediately fill you with energy. When you want to develop a spiritual experience, chant the guru mantra.

Components of a mantra

There are several components inherent in a mantra. For example, in the case of the Gayatri mantra, its seer is Rishi Vishwamitra, its devata is Surya and its vehicle is the swan. From the religious perspective, Gayatri may be considered a mantra to worship the sun god, but from the perspective of the science of vibration it activates the pranas. Awakening of the pranas creates alertness, sharpness of mind and clarity of the senses, all of which can be achieved by chanting the Gayatri mantra. This is why, in the Indian tradition, the Gayatri mantra is taught to children to enhance their intelligence and awaken their dormant talents.

Similarly, the Mahamrityunjaya mantra is chanted for the purpose of healing. The Durga mantras are chanted to overcome difficulties in life. Every mantra has a particular portfolio. It has an area of action and involvement which is predefined.

Take the example of *Lam*, the bija mantra of mooladhara chakra. In this seed vibration there is an indication of where the sound is affecting the brain and consciousness. In the image of the chakra a deity is represented, symbolizing the passive, positive, uplifting power of the mantra. In the seed sound, an animal is represented, representing the *vahana* or vehicle of the mantra.

The aggressive quality of the bija mantras is represented in the form of figures called dakinis, rakinis or shakinis. The seed sound also contains the element, or tattwa, which the particular sound influences or changes – earth, water, fire, etc. In mooladhara it is the earth element. The deity is Ganesha, the vehicle is the elephant. The lord is Brahma, the creator. These different symbols indicate the latent, inherent potential of the seed sound.

28

When chanting *Lam*, you are activating the *prithvi tattwa*, the earth element, Prithvi tattwa is solid. It is the foundation of existence – your life, house, society, family. It represents stability, security and the overcoming of fear. When you are secure, you are happy. Stability of mind is attained through repetition of the mantra *Lam*. It fixes the mind. The deity Ganesha in mooladhara is not the elephant-god, but the quality of Ganesha, a large head and a small body, representing an expanded intellect. The elephant represents strength as well as intellect. Thus, the mantra *Lam* is connected to buddhi.

Without the intellect, without intelligence, one cannot function in this world, one cannot create anything. Thus, the elephant's head is a representation of buddhi. The seed sound contains all these different ideas, in the form of its deity, its benevolent force and its confining force. The confining or limiting force of the mantra *Lam* and mooladhara is the *dakini*.

Generally people associate the term 'dakini' with demonical powers. If you ask any Indian what a dakini is, they will express fear because the image it conjures up is a very fearsome, destructive power. However, each vibration is perceived as having two roles, transcendental and gross. In the transcendental area, Ganesha is the dominant power of mooladhara, but in the gross dimension where one is confined by the senses and body, the dakini is the power which binds one to the body. These binding forces are tamasic forces, conditioning forces, and they control different areas of the gross body. For example, the dakini controls bones, and bone is an earth element; it is a structure inside the body. Therefore, the energy which creates the skeletal system utilizing the earth element, which creates a boundary around you in which you live and experience life, is the dakini's power. It is a binding power, not a liberating force. Ganesha is the liberating force, and the dakini is the force binding one to the gross material plane. These are the various aspects of the latent potential of a bija mantra. This is a brief explanation of one necessary concept of mantra, which is a vast subject.

Guru mantra and universal mantras

After the bija mantras, which are used in spiritual life to awaken different levels of consciousness, come the middle range of mantras. These are the guru mantras, which are given for one's spiritual growth, and the universal mantras, which anybody can chant at any time, anywhere. One can chant *Om Namah Shivaya, Om Namo Bhagavate Vasudevaya* or the Mahamantra – *Hare Rama Hare Rama, Rama Rama Hare Hare; Hare Krishna Hare Krishna, Krishna Krishna Hare Hare* in the form of kirtan. Whichever mantra is used to create a positive attitudinal change, an optimistic, qualitative change in the mind, falls in the middle range of mantras.

The middle range of mantras is utilized to remove stress, to focus the mind and to internalize the awareness. *Soham,* for example, is a mantra of this group, which has been used extensively in the Upanishads and the vedic traditions as a mantra to identify with one's physical and psychological states of relaxation and awareness, and to cultivate concentration and one-pointedness. With the repetition of the mantra *Soham,* one becomes receptive to higher frequency sounds and begins to hear sounds one has never heard before. The middle range of mantras sensitize the gross mind to experience the higher mind.

Kabirdas, when describing the process of ajapa japa and the mantra *Soham,* says that if you are able to repeat the mantra with every breath for twenty-four hours, you will begin to experience and hear sounds which you have not yet heard:

Aisa jap japo man layi, soham soham surta gayi;
Chhah sau sahas ikiso jap, anahad upaje aape aap.

There has to be such identification and intensity of one's awareness and concentration that one loses awareness of the external surroundings and attunes with the internal vibration. That internal vibration is *anahad,* the unheard sound.

30

Sakama mantras

In the third category or level come mantras practised for a specific purpose in material life. These mantras are now social, such as incantations and religious chants, and include mantras, stotras and prarthanas chanted for the attainment of some benefit in life, for removal of distress, acquisition of good health, knowledge or wisdom.

Misunderstanding mantras

The understanding of mantras changed as people moved further away from their spiritual nature. One example, is the meaning of the mantra *Om Namah Shivaya*. 'I salute Shiva, I bow down to Shiva,' is the literal meaning, but *Om Namah Shivaya* does not mean, 'I salute Shiva.' There are six different mantras in *Om Namah Shivaya*. First *Om*, second *Na*, third *Mah*, fourth *Shi*, fifth *Va* and sixth *Ya*. All six sounds are interconnected with different chakras. When you say *Na, Mah, Shi, Va, Ya*, you are touching different chakras. When you say the mantra *Om*, you are activating ajna chakra. When you say *Ya*, it is the heart chakra, anahata. When you say *Va*, it is swadhisthana chakra. When you say *Shi*, it is vishuddhi chakra. When you say *Namah*, it is manipura chakra. Thus these different sounds relate to different chakras, energy systems and systems of the mind. However, if you think that this is a prayer to Shiva, then you have to rethink.

Due to misunderstandings and lack of comprehension about the effects of mantras, people have associated them with religion. All the religions appeared on this planet many thousands of years after yoga. Why then were the mantras associated with religion? Why were they not kept separate as a sadhana of yoga? It is because people did not understand the intricate relationship between the body, mind and spirit.

Mantra meditative awareness
In the original system of mantra, one needs to identify with the vibration as much as possible. It is for this reason that mantras are always repeated, not chanted just once. For half an hour you are repeating the same mantra, *Om, Om, Om, Om*, or *Soham, Soham, Soham, Soham*, and nothing exists beyond this repetition. When the mantra is sustained over a period of time in this manner, for five minutes, ten minutes, fifteen minutes or half an hour, and you merge your consciousness in the feeling, chanting and articulation of the mantra, and begin to identify with the vibrations that you are creating while chanting the mantra. Then you begin to experience what is called mantra meditative awareness.

In our mantra japa, we don't experience mantra meditative awareness. The japa happens mechanically: holding the mala, moving the beads and mentally repeating one mantra per bead with the eyes closed. That is a mechanical process, it is not mantra sadhana. It is one way of involving oneself in repetition of the mantra, but not the correct way.

When you are able to sustain the mantra repetition with total awareness, to identify with the mantra vibration, to feel the mantra vibrating internally and use the mantra to deepen your own meditative awareness, then the effect will be different from mechanical repetition.

One must also realize that no mantra is less powerful or more powerful than another. A matchbox contains fifty matchsticks. Some have only a little powder so they produce a small flare and some have more powder so they produce a big flare, but the flame is the same. Does that make the matchsticks better or worse than each other? It is the quality of your intention that you put into your sadhana that is important and how deep you can go into that experience.

Three types of mantra practice
The yogic traditions have described three types of mantra practice: upanshu, baikhari and manasa. *Manasa* is mental repetition, the highest and most difficult. *Baikhari* is verbal and simplest. *Upanshu* is whispering.

Universal and *sakama*, desire-oriented, mantras can be chanted aloud. The mantras used for *anushthana*, a fixed course of sadhana, and for *aradhana*, worship, are whispered. The guru mantra and bija mantras are repeated mentally.

The best type of mantra sadhana is mental, but there is a problem. As the mind focuses, as it concentrates more and more, there is a tendency to disconnect from the world and doze off. To continuously maintain the mental awareness at the same point of mantra awareness is not possible. Ultimately, one has to come to this level of perfection in sadhana, where mantra repetition can happen with total mental attention without missing a single mantra or a single moment of awareness.

The most common form of mantra chanting is verbal. It is the primary class of mantra where you are made aware of the vibration, the sound and the pitch that you are creating, and you have to learn to sustain it and maintain continuity. After chanting verbally for some time the tendency to internalize the awareness arises automatically, and that is when the mantra begins mentally. However, internalization also creates a tendency to sleep, so at that time, in order to remain awake, you begin to whisper the mantra, you begin to move your lips. Thus the three forms of mantra chanting are verbal, whispering and mental. Mental chanting is the best, provided you can hold your awareness constantly throughout.

Open-eyed meditation

People think that meditation has to happen in the mind. That is a misconception. If you are sleeping in meditation, what is the use? You sit for one hour and for forty minutes of that hour you are nodding off, and then you claim, "I meditated for one hour." But you meditated for about half a minute, and the rest of the time you were on a trip: your mind was going here and there and then you became drowsy and went to sleep. Perfection in meditation does not happen with the eyes closed. Perfection in meditation happens with the eyes open, as you have to control, guide, analyze and cultivate the intensity of your awareness. You should not be blocking the intensity or reducing the level of your awareness. If you reduce the level of awareness in meditation , then you sleep.

When Sri Swamiji was teaching me pratyahara and other practices in the late 1960s, he did not teach me in a classroom environment but in a very spontaneous way. He would be working away, answering letters and so on, and he would say to me, "Go and stand in the sun there and watch your shadow for ten minutes, and then tell me what you are seeing." He would ask me to go and do something else for five or fifteen minutes and then tell him the experience. That is how I was trained.

The way Sri Swamiji trained me was very simple, natural and spontaneous. I did not even feel that I was doing anything. He gave me guidelines and hints: "Go and meditate with your eyes open." I did not understand it then, but today I do. If I ask you to meditate with your eyes open, you will not be able to.

34

The real mantra sadhana

The point is very simple. We have to move from the verbal and wakeful state to the mental and internal state in mantra. Begin with repetition of the mantra first and attain mastery over that for one mala. See if you can sustain that awareness for five minutes. Practise this until you complete one mala. Then double the time, to two malas, sustain the awareness for ten minutes, with the same intensity and concentration. Then increase it to three malas and increase the time accordingly. In this way, gradually keep on increasing the attention span. Once the attention span increases to at least half an hour, then you experience the inner mantra, which vibrates within. This is the real mantra sadhana. Prior to that is training to increase the attention span.

For the last forty years I have been training myself, as I've told you before. Sri Swamiji asked me to do one mala. I thought one mala would only take five minutes, so I should do more. He said, "No, do one mala with absolute awareness," and I am still trying to do that. I am proud of what I have achieved.

Only when the attention span has increased can one move into the experience of the mantra. One cannot move into the experience of the mantra instantaneously, just by repeating or chanting.

In summary

The important aspects of today's discussions are that mantras are grouped in to three categories: spiritually uplifting and awakening mantras which are the bija mantras, the middle range of mantras, which connect the lower mind with the higher mind, and the lower group of mantras to fulfil our whims and desires. Eighty percent of people who practise mantra belong to this lower category: "I'm sick, I'm suffering so I'm practising mantra. I have this desire or problem and I want to fulfil or manage it, so I'm practising mantra. I'm distressed so I start practising mantra."

When people stay at the ashram for some time, they begin to understand that the purpose of mantra is to move from the lower mind to the higher mind. Such people can spend ten or twelve more years in the ashram, trying to develop that movement from the lower to the higher mind.

The higher application of the mantra is given to the appropriate person by the appropriate teacher, so there is no use talking about it. In this higher realm, the mantra actually becomes a map of your own consciousness, and is realized as a yantra.

Yantras: Maps of Consciousness

19th March 2010

The basic concept of mantra is that it is *nada*, subtle sound vibration, which is the first manifestation of energy. It is a frequency of vibration, a frequency of consciousness and a frequency of energy. We perceive these three components in a mantra: the natural vibration of the nada, the evolute principle; the natural nada of the conscious faculty, self-acknowledgement; and the natural *spandan*, vibrations, of the energy faculty. These vibrations bring about a transformation in the normal sensorial human personality by sensitizing the

mind and awareness to experience the subtle inherent flows of energy. Mantras are used to deepen concentration and to access the deeper realms of the mind.

Upon accessing the deeper realms of the mind, at first we are the observer, the *drashta*, and after having observed and realized these inner states we become the experiencer, the *bhokta*, of these experiences. With mantras we begin to see the subtle levels that exist within the dimensions of consciousness and energy. Once there is an understanding and an awareness of the vibrational dimension, we begin to experience it. The whole body begins to vibrate with that inner spandan, the mind vibrates with it. That is the experience of anandamaya kosha.

Symbols of consciousness

Mantras also have a form, a shape, called a yantra. It is believed that every thought has a form, every emotion, every desire, every mental expression has a form. These forms are sensorial in nature. Anything that is created by the mind is recognized by the senses and is sensorial in nature. Through your eyes you see a form, the faculty of vision is actively recognizing that form. You hear a sound, the ears pick it up, they are actively recognizing the sound. Each sense organ, while expressing its potential, indicates that there is a deep and intense sensory connection of the mind and gross senses with whatever we are experiencing. To move out of this sensory connection and identification is very difficult, because the moment you do that, you lose body awareness. Yantras indicate a process of knowing and realizing by which one can overcome this sensorial body identification. Yantras are subtle archetypes, the inner symbols of consciousness.

First level of symbols: sensory inputs

In the early days of modern psychology, Jung spoke about the symbols of consciousness. He identified those symbols as different images that we perceive in times of relaxation, or sleep, or in the form of memories, recollections and dreams.

38

He called them symbols of the unconscious. But today, when we begin to analyze the symbols of consciousness, we discover that they have many levels and layers of experiences.

The first symbols to be realized, seen or visualized are sensory experiences which the mind perceives in the form of symbols. Often people relive the events of the day or of the past in dreams. The events or memories that leave their definite impressions in the consciousness, are called archetypes. These are sensory archetypes, and during sleep something triggers them so that the sleeper begins to see them as dreams. Sometimes a thought is enough to trigger them, sometimes a particular stress level in the personality is enough to trigger a recollection of an event. Whatever we see, first is the sensory input. That is the first level of symbols.

The senses communicate through speech and through movement. We communicate through speech and movement. I am talking and at the same time I am moving my hands. You are listening and you are watching this movement. All our life we express ourselves by speech and movement in order to recognize, connect or describe our perceptions to others. Speech and movement become the archetypes of the senses in the unconscious mind. Everything that is experienced is being stored in the unconscious, like in the hard drive of a computer.

Whatever we store in a computer remains there till we retrieve it. However, even if we delete the information and clean the entire hard drive, it is still possible to extract the deleted information from a blank or a cleaned hard drive. The information remains in the form of electronic, laser or magnetic impressions or some other form. In the same manner, it is not possible for a person to fully delete everything from the mind as some impressions will always remain. Therefore, even though you may believe you overcame a situation many months or years ago, it will suddenly flash before you and you will again experience the same memory and emotion, sentiment, feeling, thought or mood. From where did it come, something you thought you had worked through? Suddenly you realize that the remnant, the tail, is still there, and that is the archetype. The memories, visual inputs and sensory inputs, become archetypes.

Non-verbal symbols

Another range of symbols is non-verbal. Non-verbal symbols are beyond the scope and range of the senses and represent the building blocks of the personality. They are not what we receive, understand or analyze through the senses but what we have come with in this life in the form of our character, nature, behaviour, personality, attitude and mentality.

As a person, you came with certain qualities and limitations. Those qualities evolve and the limitations also evolve. You experience yourself now with both your shortcomings

40

and strengths. However, you don't know what your strengths or shortcomings are until you recognize the archetypes or samskaras which have made your personality what it is now.

Transcendental symbols

The third group of archetypes is trans-sensorial and transcendental. They are the maps of consciousness, *yantras*, geometric forms that were visualized by yogis in deep states of meditation when they tried to experience and understand the subtle vibrations within their own bodies and the cosmos. What they heard were mantras and what they saw were yantras. At this level of consciousness the impressions or symbols are trans-sensorial perceptions.

Yantras were also seen when the yogis tried to visualize the formless Supreme Element. What is the vision of formlessness? It is when, instead of an imagined material form, you experience its essential element. It is that which has not assumed a material form as yet, nevertheless it exists. Tantra explains that the shivalingam is the symbolic representation of the formless Shiva, while the image of Shiva as a person, wearing a tiger skin, with snakes coiled around his neck, the Ganga flowing from his locks, is the representation of his manifest form. In the same way, the image of Durga as a goddess is the representation of the manifest form of that aspect, but the Durga yantra symbolizes the formless Durga.

Yantras are symbols of the formless transcendental reality. How can you imagine that which is nothing? How will you contemplate that which you have never seen? What is the formless representation of water? H_2 and O; two parts hydrogen and one part oxygen. When the two unite, they become water whose form you can see. When they are separate, you cannot see them with the naked eye. In this case, the formula is the formless representation. In the same way, a yantra is a symbolic representation of the eternal principle.

Yantras can also appear in dreams when the mind has bypassed the senses and gross physical awareness.

Tools for transformation

In the Indian tradition, the use of mantra and yantra is synonymous with bhakti sadhana, as mantra and yantra channel and purify the emotions and create a state of mind in which the aspirant can connect with the object of worship, the *ishta*.

Bhakti is a state of mind. There are different states of mind – jealousy, hatred, love, compassion, greed, arrogance, etc. Similarly, bhakti is also a state of mind. The other states of mind connect one to the material world, whereas bhakti connects one with one's object of inner identification.

The scriptures have defined bhakti in many ways. In the *Bhagavad Gita*, Sri Krishna describes bhakti as a process of positive and qualitative transformation of one's mental, attitudinal life. In fact, all the statements on bhakti emphasize the need to arrest the dissipations of the mind and focus it on the object of one's identification. The final state of bhakti is *atma nivedan*, surrender of the self. But its initial stage is positive and qualitative transformation of the gross, lower mind. This is achieved with the help of mantras and yantras, as they create a connection with the Supreme Element.

Configuration of yantras

Yantras are geometric configurations, mainly constructed of triangles and circles within a framework of squares. The basic geometric figure in the yantra is the line. From

42

the yogic and tantric perspective, a line is the only way of expressing the unknown. It is the symbol of space. From the line emerge triangles. There are two kinds of triangles in yantras: inverted and upright. The inverted triangle represents energy and the upright triangle represents consciousness.

In the inverted triangle, the horizantal line above represents space, the left line moving downward represents time and the right line moving downward represents object. Space, time and object: that which is recognized by the individual and lived in by the individual. We are living in the dimension of time, space and object, and that is the dimension of Shakti, represented by the inverted triangle. Space on top, time moving down and sense object awareness moving down. Thus the inverted triangle becomes the symbol of Shakti.

43

The chakra system also represents this downward movement of energy, from transcendental to gross; down from sahasrara, down through the different chakras, to mooladhara. This downward movement is towards what is binding, constricting and confining. You are coming down into a confined state of senses, mind, consciousness and energy.

The upright triangle of consciousness is defined in the opposite way. The flat line representing space is at the bottom, and the lines of time and object extend up and meet in space. When the Shakti principle, the inverted triangle, is active, then from the transcendental or pure level of existence we come down to the confined, lower level. When consciousness becomes active, the process reverses. Now our yogic and spiritual journey is upward. The kundalini rises from mooladhara and goes up to sahasrara. The upward journey is towards freedom and the downward journey is towards bondage. The triangles represent that journey.

The circle is another component of the yantra. It represents the wheel of life, the circle of life and death. In life and in death it is the vibrant archetypes of yantras that take us beyond our present state to higher levels of evolution. Thus, the wheel of life and death becomes the dimension in which the progression or regression of consciousness and energy is perceived, identified and experienced.

Visualization of yantra

In the state of deep concentration the visualization of yantras creates a powerful energy field in the mind. Those who practise *trataka*, fixed gazing, on a candle flame will know that the practice makes the mind still. Even insomniacs can go to sleep easily if they practise trataka properly. The mind becomes totally focused on the symbol and the mental attitude and mood changes completely. Trataka is visual and mental. When you begin to visualize the yantra internally, when the yantra appears in your mind spontaneously, you are entering another dimension of consciousness. It is like moving from the waking state to the dreaming state, from the dreaming state to the pranic state, from the pranic state to the sleeping state.

The movement from the waking state to the dreaming state indicates an altered state of consciousness. You are living in the dreaming state, what your senses and mind have experienced in the waking state. In the same manner, when you focus on the yantra, an altered state of consciousness is perceived.

No one has complete clarity about the use of yantras. However, those who have applied an understanding of yantra in their respective fields have gained many creative benefits. In Switzerland and France experiments with yantras were conducted on school children. A yantra colouring book was distributed to young students. For three to six months in their art classes, they were asked to colour in only the yantras and not the things which they normally would have, like houses, trees, mountains, rivers, the sun, the moon, etc.

The children were seeing the yantra symbols continuously and the visualization of the yantra symbols was altering the dissipated pattern in their mind. The task of colouring the yantras acted as a meditative process, as the children had to focus on the yantra in order to colour it in. The effects became evident after three or four months when their grasping, retentive and expressive abilities showed a major improvement compared with other children who were painting in normal colouring books. Dr Jacques Coulon in Switzerland wrote a book in which he states that by painting yantras, the children's powers of retention, ability to grasp information and creative expression show an upward incline.

Finding your yantra

By focusing on the image of a yantra, an external symbol, it is possible to access one's own yantra, as the practitioner enters into a deeper level of the mind.

In order to discover your own yantra, the map of consciousness, start with something simple, just a dot. Let the yantra build itself up from that. The yantra which builds up naturally reflects your state of evolution at that given moment.

Often, people just select a yantra because they like it and are attracted to it, and start practising sadhana. You know that the Sri Yantra is a powerful shakti yantra so you use it in meditation. You sit there cross-eyed looking at the Sri Yantra for months and then you distance yourself. You enjoyed the practice for a few minutes, you felt calm and peaceful, but that was not your yantra. You went cross-eyed in the belief that yantra meditation was going to change your psyche and life instantly!

Yantras are maps of consciousness that emerge as you meditate. They are an indication of your progress and growth, and your limitations, blocks and impediments. Yantras are tools of meditation. Yantra actually means an instrument, an apparatus. It is a tool of meditation, a tool for accessing the unconscious, and through the unconscious the superconscious.

Mantra and Yantra:
An Internal Havan

20th March 2010

Yantra means an instrument, a medium by which one can access the deeper layers of consciousness. Yantras are geometrical patterns, geometrical symbols which represent the movement of energy within consciousness. Several different geometric figures are used in the creation of yantras.

The square of four gates

The first figure is the square, which is the outline of the yantra. The square represents the material world, the entire creative world, with the four directions of north, east, south and west. It represents the world within which we exist at present, the world of senses and sense objects. This world or square has four entrances which are called *dwara*, portals. The portals represent manas, buddhi, chitta and ahamkara. These four components of the mind are the agents through which one functions and survives in the sensorial world. All the knowledge, perceptions and experiences of the world are derived either from buddhi, chitta, manas or ahamkara. They are the gateways to experience existence or life. That is the first level of a yantra: the square with four doors.

The circle of timelessness

Often on top, and often within the framework of the square there is a circle, which represents timelessness, continuity, the cycle of birth and death. Whether you believe in reincarnation or not, birth and death are cosmic realities. Your acceptance or rejection of the idea does not change the reality which has governed the universe from time immemorial. Therefore, what we believe changes all the time, but not the permanent reality which transcends all beliefs, ideas and speculations.

The circle represents timelessness and the cycle of birth and death. Sri Shankaracharya says in the stotra 'Mohamudgar':

Punarapi jananam, punarapi maranam; punarapi janani jathare shayanam

Many times are we born, many times do we die; many times we have slept in the womb of the mother.

For what purpose? To realize our true essential nature. Until one realizes one's true nature, one is caught in the cycle of birth and death. Only after such realization can one be free from this cycle of birth and death. This freedom is the state of a *jivanmukta*, one who has become free from the attractions and bondages of life.

Swami Satyananda's example

If you look at Swami Satyananda's life, you will find that it is divided into twenty-year cycles. He lived at home until he was twenty, then his spiritual quest started. He lived with his guru and as a parivrajaka from twenty-one to forty, from 1943 to 1963. Thereafter he worked to fulfil the mandate of his guru, the propagation of yoga, which he did for another cycle of twenty years, from 1963 to 1983. He was ready to leave in 1983, but then I appeared on the scene and requested him, "Please stay at Ganga Darshan for a few more years to teach me." He said, "All right, I will give you five years of my time." Therefore, from 1983 to 1988 he gave his personal time to me, at Ganga Darshan. Then, in 1989 he went to Rikhia, and the Rikhia chapter was also twenty years, from 1989 to 2009.

48

In the life that Sri Swamiji lived, many of us have witnessed him as a teacher, a guru, an enlightened being, as a siddha, and we all had our own personal relationship with him. However, what makes me aware of his spirituality is his lifestyle. When I observe his life, and I have been lucky enough to observe him closely right from the early days, I discover that in 2003 he became free of all karmas. Not a single karma remained in his life which he needed to work for, fulfil or accomplish. On several occasions he said to us, "If you hear me say something, remember it, because I am not going to repeat those words again. I am cleaning my memory of all impressions. I am wiping my hard drive." In this manner he actually wiped clear his mind of everything, his desires, his aspirations, his ambitions, and became free from all karmas. From 2003 to 2009 he lived as a *jivanmukta*, one who has transcended body awareness and mental limitations. He was living the state of the highest spiritual attainment, where the mind is totally subdued and the awareness is fixed on higher consciousness.

I am telling you this to explain that in order to access the deeper levels of the mind one has to eliminate the accumulated stuff. Only when one has removed everything can one claim that he or she is free from bondage. If there is a pending desire at the time of death, then you are not free from the bondages of life. Life still has an attraction for you.

The circle of life and death

Bondage in life is represented by the circle of the yantra, the cyclical continuation of life and death, the endless cycle of life and death. When one is able to liberate oneself from gross sensorial involvement, attractions and identifications, one can identify with one's inner nature, and then one becomes free from worldly bondage and attraction to sense objects.

From the tantric perspective, life and death are two sides of the same coin. When you come into this life, the other side follows. If you are born, you will die. If you die, you will be born. You know that if you are born, you will die at the end of your time. You don't need to read philosophy or to be educated for that, it is a reality. However, what one has not seen, and therefore does not believe, is that everybody who dies takes birth again. That is also a reality. Religions may or may not believe in reincarnation. Philosophies may or may not believe in it, but the cycle of birth and death is a cosmic reality.

Tantra says that life and death are continuous processes. One keeps coming back again and again. Nature has put a bolt and a lock on the door which contains the memories, experiences and awareness of past lives. This is done with a purpose. If one were to begin to remember the past, one would become crazy. Therefore, Nature has done a good job of locking the door of the memories retained from previous births.

The circle of the yantra represents this continuous process of birth and death, and the rotation of consciousness and energy in every birth. That rotation of consciousness and energy in every life is evolution, which is maturity of consciousness.

Interlaced triangles of Shiva and Shakti

Inside the circle of the yantra there are triangles. The inverted triangle pointing downwards represents Shakti, the power which is descending and confining itself into a perceivable identity: the body, the world, objects. This Shakti is the controller of time, space and object. Consciousness is identified with the upright triangle, the ascending consciousness.

In the yantras these two triangles interlace or merge together, indicating the play of consciousness and energy. This means that while one is living in this material dimension, there exists the possibility of one's ascent to spiritual realms, higher realms. If one is unable to harness that power of consciousness and energy, one's nature becomes materialistic and is bound by the influence of the sense objects, by pleasure and comfort, acquisition and satisfaction. However, while one lives in this world where one desires everything for oneself, there is also the possibility of transcending the gross level and experiencing the ascent of consciousness back to the point, the source.

Thus, one of the two interlaced triangles is pointing downwards, representing the physical world, and the other is pointing upwards, representing transcendental union. In Prakriti, time and object come together to give life, and in *chetana*, consciousness, time and object disappear. There is manifestation at the lower level and merger at the higher level. The placement of the triangles within the yantra represents the flow of energy during specific mental states or conditions.

Representations of energy movement

The energy expressions are different when one is angry, when one is afraid, when one is aggressive and when one is peaceful. They change at different times because of the mood. The mood reflects the change in the behaviour pattern or state of passive consciousness and passive energy. If consciousness and energy are passive, you will be calm and quiet. But if a spike is experienced in the dimension of consciousness or energy, at the point you will feel distraction, disturbance and agitation. The moods of our mind reflect the change of energy flow in the shakti systems. The cause may be external or internal, but where energy is altered, your perceptions change.

The placement of various triangles within the circle represents the movement of energy in different levels of experience. For example, when you are angry, the energy is dynamic and vibrant, but when you meditate, the energy is smooth and passive. When you are feeling passion the energy becomes dynamic and aggressive; when you are in a positive environment, the energy becomes peaceful. We attribute that to our likes and dislikes, the mind, senses, desires and expectations. Whatever the cause, the flow of energy and awareness have both changed.

The triangles in the yantras represent the flow of energy. If a yantra has three triangles, it means that three levels of energy are being dealt with. If the yantra has twenty triangles, it means that one has to realize twenty levels of mental behaviour or states of consciousness. Each triangle represents either a major or minor alteration in the frequency of consciousness and energy. Different symbols represent different activities that take place in the depths of the unconscious at the level of instincts, samskaras, karmas and destiny.

In the centre of the yantra is the point, the *bindu*. The bindu is the seat and focal point of the power that governs and controls the yantra that one is focusing on.

The yantra becomes the plate on which the fire of mantra is kindled. In a havan a yantra is drawn on the havan plate, depending on the result one wants to achieve. The yantra is not chosen on a whim or due to its beauty. If that were done, then the whole purpose would be lost. When you go to school, you have to study all the subjects, irrespective of whether you like them or not. If you negate something which you don't like or don't feel inspired by, it is due to your own lack of understanding. In the case of a yantra, if you go by your whims, you are negating the spiritual composition of forces and energies.

Yantra represents the energy of a particular quality of power. Each yantra, according to its combination of circles, squares, triangles, hexagons, pentagons, etc., represents either a masculine or a feminine power. The masculine power represents the power of consciousness, *devata*, and the feminine power represents the power of cosmic energy, *devi*. Thus, there are Shiva yantras and Shakti yantras. Both use triangles, squares and other geometric patterns, but their placement is such that they became the focal point for different powers. When you concentrate or gaze on a yantra, that image is captured by the camera of the subconscious mind.

Our subconscious mind is continuously capturing pictures and images even though our conscious mind recognizes only a few based on its focus at a given moment. I am looking at you, but I know that my mind is picking up pictures of the trees that I can see in the periphery of my vision. The shape of the trees is being registered by the mind although I am not aware of them. I am not even watching them, but my mind is capturing that information. Therefore, when you look at a

53

yantra, it may not mean much to you, but it means a lot to the energy patterns of your mind. These inner energy patterns begin to respond to concentration and awareness when you meditate on a yantra, as those images create powerful psychological impressions.

Developing the intuitive mind

As I was telling you earlier, children experience enhanced creativity by colouring in yantras without even understanding what they are. Every child knows: 'I am painting a house, a tree or the sun.' The intellectual thought is there. But when they colour a yantra, what can they think of? It is not a house, scenery or a person. It is not identifiable. It is only squares and triangles and circles. However, just concentration on the image affects and improves intuitive and creative thinking.

Intuitive thinking occurs as flashes. Malcom Gladwell, in his book *Blink* (Penguin, London, 2005), gives the example of an investigation into the authenticity of a famous sculpture. In 1983 an art dealer approached the J. Paul Getty Museum in California, with what he said was a Greek 6th century BC marble statue. It was a well-known but rare sculpture, known as kouros, of which there were only about two hundred in the world. The statues that had been already discovered were either severely damaged or relics from archaeological finds, but this statue was in perfect condition. After fourteen months of detailed and scientific examination into the authenticity of the sculpture, the museum agreed to buy it. and it went on display in 1986.

However, during its time at the museum, the sculpture came under further scrutiny. To some experts, in spite of its validation, it just didn't look right. One art historian found himself inexplicably drawn to the fingertips of the statue which seemed wrong to him. To one expert, when she viewed the statue, immediately there was a feeling that something was amiss, but she didn't know what. The first response in the mind of another was that the statue looked

'fresh' – not an appropriate response to a genuine 2,000 year-old statue.

The museum called a meeting of experts in Greece, and shipped the sculpture to Athens to have it investigated further. There, it met with even stronger criticism. One expert felt that he was looking at the statue through glass. Another could tell it had never been in the ground. Another felt 'intuitive repulsion' towards it. Eventually, it was discovered that the statue was a forgery. The intuitive responses turned out to be the correct ones rather than the museum's fourteen months of legal and scientific investigations. Those first responses were feelings that no one could explain, a feeling of just knowing. Those first thoughts are intuitions, those you cannot rationalize.

Concentration on yantras develops intuitive as well as creative ability. Intuition means that you are already connected with whatever you need to know; a connection already exists. Intuition is real. It works strongly between mother and child. If the child is in another location and falls ill, the mother begins to feel uncomfortable and memories of the child flash although she doesn't know that her child is sick. That intuitive feeling comes, the memory and remembrance comes and she phones her child to see if everything is all right.

Combined force of mantra and yantra

Many years ago I read that the vibration of the bija mantra of Devi, *Hrim*, and of the mantra *Om* of the Vedas are the same. At that time I did not understand, as, after all, they are two different sounds and are pronounced differently. Years later, during my global travels, I saw an instrument which created pictures based on the vibrations of audible sound. I started chanting the mantra *Om* before the instrument. The picture that emerged after some time was that of the Sri Yantra, and the bija mantra of the Sri Yantra is *Hrim*!

Yantras bypass the mental or intellectual level; they exert an influence at the level of chitta and ahamkara. Mantras act at the level of manas and buddhi, and open the lock of chitta and ahamkara. Manas and buddhi are the areas of mantra and to explore the realms of chitta and ahamkara you need the yantra. Both become very powerful tools for internal enlightenment. Therefore, mantra and yantra are the most important components of tantra. When you have the right yantra and practise the corresponding mantra, the effect doubles. For example, if you are chanting a Shiva mantra, *Om Namah Shivaya*, and you have the Shiva yantra placed before you, and simultaneously practise trataka on it, the experience will be very intense. But first one has to work through the gross levels of the mind.

Sri Swamiji gives the example that if you run 440 volts of current through a wire which is capable of carrying only 220 volts, the wire will burn out. In every building there are switches, lights and fans, but they all function at only 220 volts. If 440 volts is supplied through those wires, the fuses will blow. Similarly, this structure of ours is wired for 220 volts of energy which flows through manas, buddhi, chitta and ahamkara. Our body is conditioned to accept only 220 volts. That is the capacity of the senses, the nerves and the brain circuits. In order to increase the potency of the current, one has to work through the gross first.

Mantra and yantra together become an internal havan. On the plate of consciousness and energy you are lighting the fire of mantra. That is the tantric concept of sadhana, but tantric teachings are not given openly as people are not ready to receive these higher teachings. Therefore, during these four days I have given you a glimpse into the concept of mantra and yantra, according to the tantric perspective. With this awareness you can begin to modify your understanding and approach to your spiritual development. In this way you can definitely go very far and that will be your achievement in this life.